© Aladdin Books Ltd

Designed and produced by
Aladdin Books Ltd
70 Old Compton Street
LONDON W1

First published in the
United States in 1987 by
Gloucester Press
387 Park Avenue South
New York NY 10016

ISBN 0 531 17048 9

Certain illustrations originally published in
The Closer Look Series

Bees and Wasps

Contents

Bees and Wasps

Kate Petty

Illustrated by
Tony Swift and Norman Weaver

small world

Gloucester Press

New York · London · Toronto · Sydney

Looking at bees and wasps

Have you ever watched bees as they
buzz from flower to flower?
They sip nectar from deep inside
the flower with their long tongues.
Nectar is sugary liquid that
the bees turn into honey.

Bumblebees gathering nectar

Some bees collect fine yellow dust on
their back legs. It is called pollen.
Some of the pollen drops off onto
other flowers. It fertilizes them
so they can produce
seeds. This is called
pollination.

Honeybee

The Honeybee

Some kinds of bees live on their own,
but Honeybees live in nests with
many other bees.
They build their nests in hollow
trees or under rocks.
Bee-keepers keep Honeybees in beehives
and collect their honey.

Bees nesting
in the wild

A beehive

There is one queen bee in each nest.
She is the largest. She lays the eggs.
Male bees are called drones.
One of them will mate with the queen
but the others don't do anything.
Female bees are the workers.
They gather food and look after the nest.

A Honeybee worker

antennae

sting

tongue

hairy legs
for collecting
pollen

Starting a new nest

When there are too many bees in a nest
the queen and about half the bees fly
off to look for a new one.
This is called swarming.
The workers cluster around the queen.

Bees swarming

The workers build a new nest together.
They form a chain called a
"wax garland" and shape cells with wax
from their bodies.
The queen starts to lay eggs in the
new cells right away.

A wax garland

These bees are
receiving "queen
substance" from
the queen.
It helps them
to recognize
their own nest.

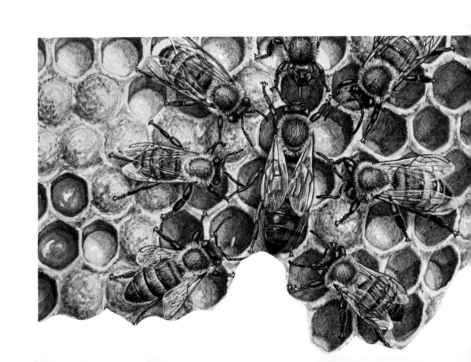

Only one queue

Only one queen

Before leaving the old nest
the queen bee lays a few eggs
in special queen cells.
The larvae in the queen cells are fed
on "royal jelly" rather than honey.
Now a princess is hatching.
If another one hatches the queen bee
kills it.

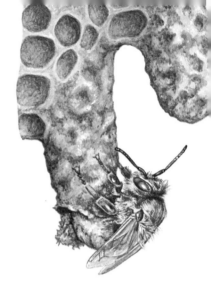

The princess
will become
the new queen

The new queen killing
a rival

On the tenth day of her life, the
princess takes off on her mating flight.
The drones swarm after her.
One of them mates with her.
Now she can lay eggs.
The other drones are no use to the nest
any more. At the end of summer
the workers push them out.

Worker bees
push out
the drones
at the end
of summer

The life of a Honeybee worker
In this picture you can see a worker Honeybee
that has just hatched from her cell (1).
At first she begs for honey from the
older workers (2).
After three days she can feed herself
on honey and pollen (3).
Now she can help to feed the growing
grubs.

Bees in the nest

Young workers
feed the grubs
with nectar
and pollen.

They store nectar
gathered by
the older bees.

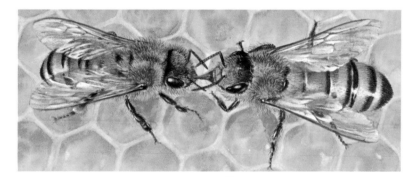

After three weeks
they can fly out
and gather nectar
and pollen and
water for themselves.
Workers born in
the summer only live
for five or six weeks.

A hive of activity

This picture shows you what goes on inside a honeybees' nest.
It might contain 30,000 bees.

The queen lays eggs in the cells (1).
They hatch into larvae (grubs) about three days later (2).
Workers feed the larvae (3).
After nine days the larvae are sealed in their cells (4).
The larvae weave cocoons around themselves. Now they are called pupae.
The pupa becomes a bee (5).
The worker bee soon starts work. This one is storing pollen (6). Can you see what the other worker bees are doing?

A princess is hatching. Maybe the old queen is about to leave the nest.

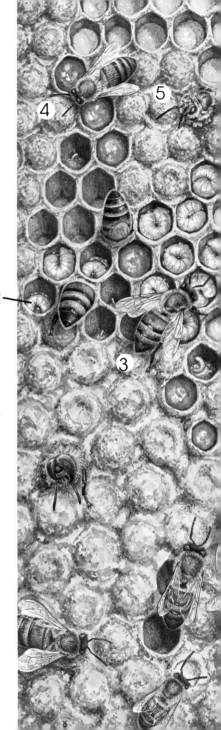

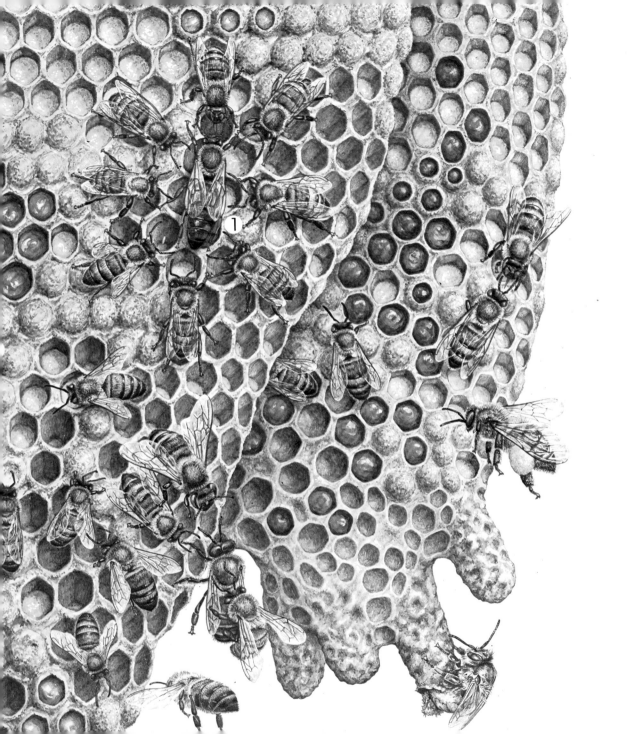

Bumblebee

A queen
hibernates
in winter

Bumblebees

All Bumblebees are furry.
They can survive in cold northern
countries. They live together in
nests that last for one summer.
At the end of the summer the queen
mates.
The other Bumblebees die, and the
queen sleeps through the winter.
When spring comes she starts to build
her nest alone. She might use the old
nest of a fieldmouse.
She lays about ten eggs in an egg cell.
When the eggs hatch, the new worker
Bumblebees help her build more cells
for more eggs.

By late summer there will be about 500
Bumblebees in the nest. The queen is tired now.
She lays some eggs that will become queens
and males. Soon she and all the workers will die.

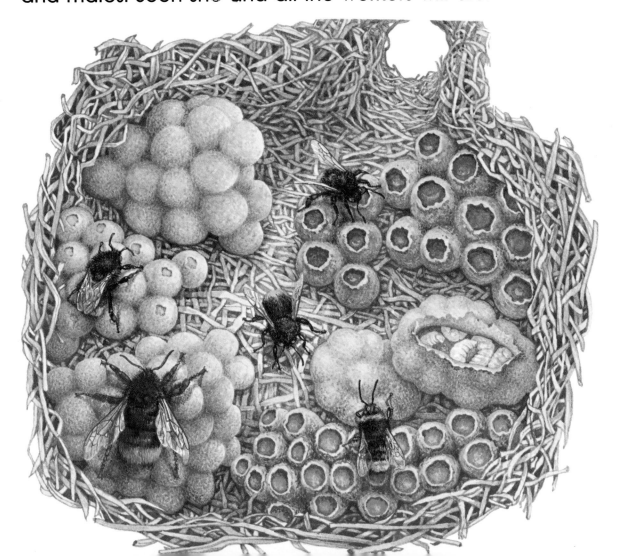

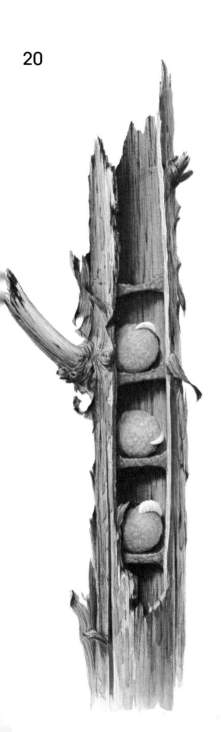

Different bees, different nests

Some kinds of bees live alone. They are called solitary bees.

The females make nests only to lay their eggs in. They store pollen for the grubs to feed on but they don't make honey. Solitary bees build their nests in some very strange places.

Carpenter bees get their name because they lay their eggs in hollow wood. They separate the cells with chewed-up pulp. Carpenter bees live in tropical countries.

If you see leaves with bites taken
out of them, it could be because
the Leafcutter bee is at work.
She rolls a leaf-tube for each egg,
and cuts a perfect fitting
lid for the top.
Leafcutters often nest in hollow stems
but sometimes the leaf tubes are found
in empty snail shells.

Leafcutter bees

The common wasp or Yellowjacket
You can tell that wasps and bees belong
to the same family by their double pairs of
transparent wings and their "wasp waists."
Unlike bees, wasps feed on other insects.
They paralyze or kill them with their stings.
The wasp you see most often is called the
Yellowjacket. After sleeping through the winter
the queen starts to build her nest alone.
The grubs hang upside down in the nest.
As new workers hatch, they feed the grubs on
chewed-up insects.

Yellowjacket wasp

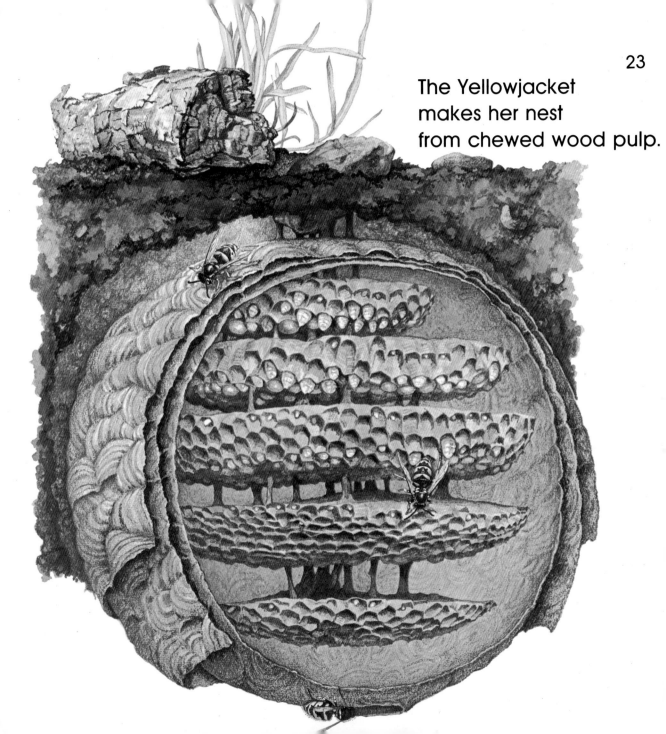

The Yellowjacket makes her nest from chewed wood pulp.

Solitary hunters

Solitary wasps have to provide live insects
for their grubs to feed on. They build some
very unusual nests for the eggs and their food.
The Potter wasp's nest is like a mud pot.
She pushes a paralyzed caterpillar inside,
lays her egg on it and closes the top.
When the grub hatches it feeds on
the caterpillar.

Potter wasp

The Spider wasp catches a spider by
stinging and paralyzing it. Then she
digs a burrow, puts the spider inside
and lays her egg on it. Each egg has to
have one spider. Some of these wasps
capture tarantulas.

Spider wasp

Wasps without stings

These wasps have no "wasp waists" and no stings.
Instead, they have a long tube for laying eggs,
called an ovipositor.
The Wood wasp drills its eggs into a treetrunk.
When the larvae (grubs) hatch they can move
about like caterpillars.
Wood wasp grubs feed on the wood and burrow out.

Wood wasp

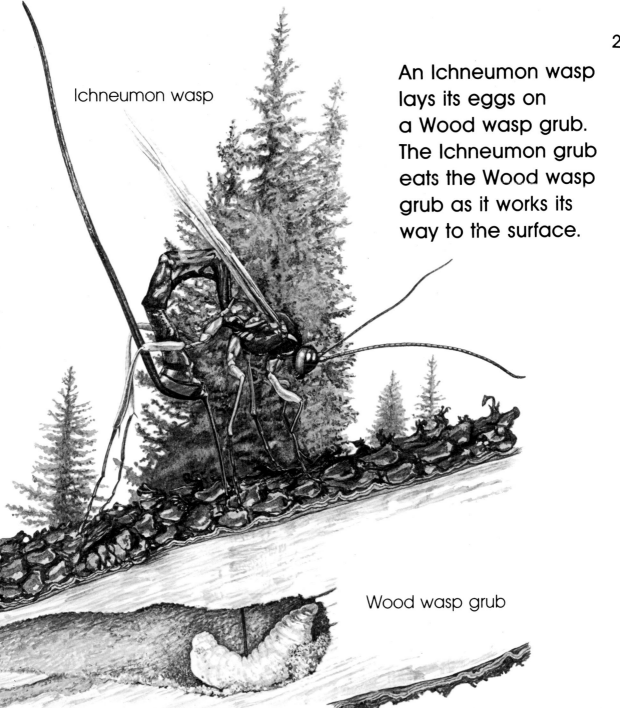

Ichneumon wasp

An Ichneumon wasp
lays its eggs on
a Wood wasp grub.
The Ichneumon grub
eats the Wood wasp
grub as it works its
way to the surface.

Wood wasp grub

Why we need bees

Wasps and bees are useful creatures.
Wasps help to control insect pests.
Bees give us honey and wax.
But the most important job they do is to
pollinate our flowering plants.
Without them we would have no wild flowers
and no beautiful gardens.

Index

PRINTED IN BELGIUM BY
proost
INTERNATIONAL BOOK PRODUCTION